Copyright © 2020 by Matt Bodett

All rights reserved. This book or any portion thereof may not be reproduced or used in any manner whatsoever without the express written permission of the publisher except for the use of brief quotations in a book review and certain other noncommercial uses permitted by copyright law. For permission requests, write to the publisher at the address below.

Printed in the United States of America

First Printing, 2020

ISBN: 978-1-7347545-3-7

Press Here
410 S Michigan Ave Suite 420
Chicago, IL 60605

www.mattbodett.com

two tragedies

songs for eleven masks and a play for a bell jar

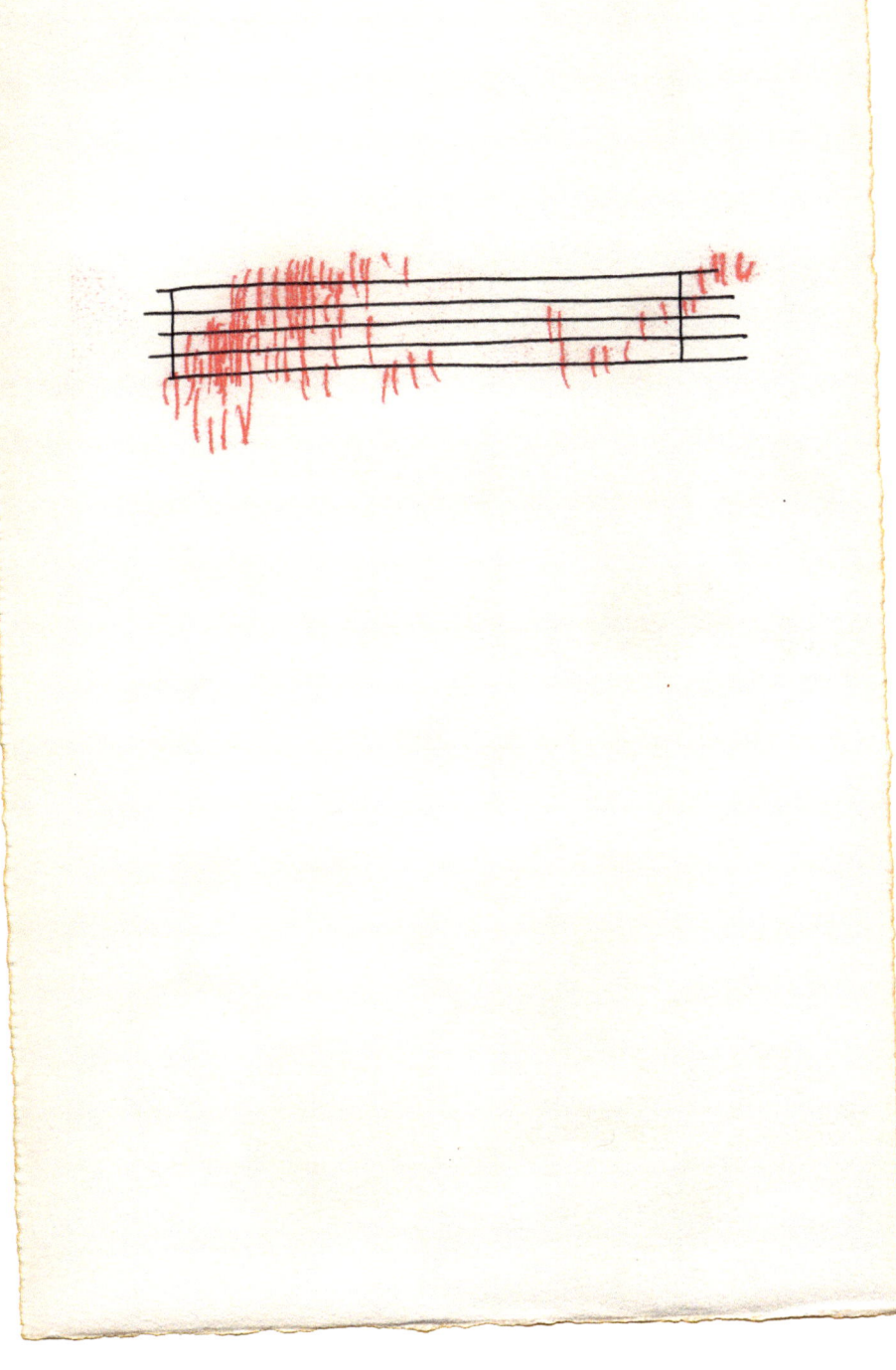

a play for a bell jar

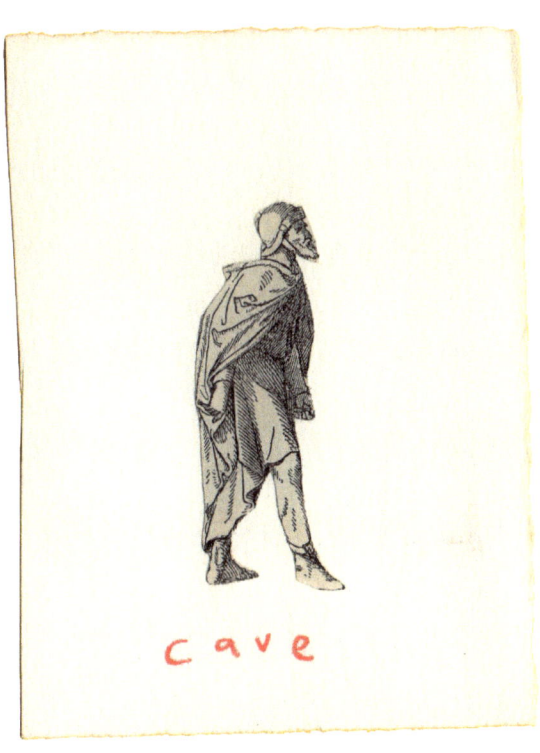
cave

collector

chorus

~~poet~~
cook

validate

disappear

I will
be
leaving

You are in here

It is
subtle
to
believe

ring
ing

shatt
er

I've written essays

hey

hey

hey

It's
an
all
egory

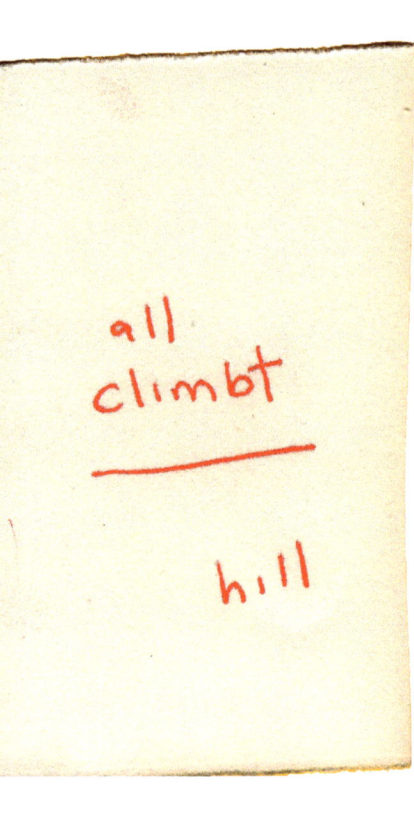

with
ragg

its all
like
seasons
and
for
crying

$$\frac{\text{alone}+}{\text{in every}}$$

yoursmade

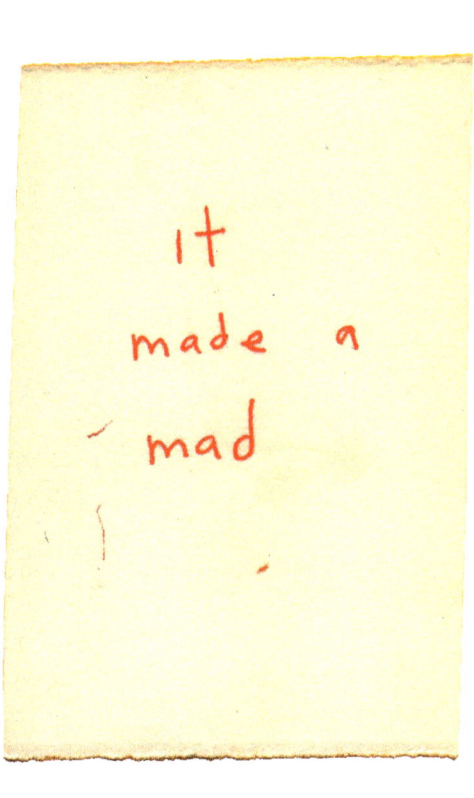

you can
be
taught
grief

lft
maket
dayst

it's
settled —
 like
 dust

sweeping

I really
should know

let's
go
for a
ride
---
sait

pouring
water
in
a
tin
can

"for the first time i ~~feeling~~ understood it was possible to reach the under~~side~~ of surface the tangible horizon..."

don't
leave

all
of
time

www.ingramcontent.com/pod-product-compliance
Lightning Source LLC
Chambersburg PA
CBHW040926190426
43197CB00033B/109